OUR

Engagement

JOURNAL

....

and

....

OUR
Engagement
JOURNAL

Amy Elliott

LONDON · NEW YORK

CONTENTS

INTRODUCTION

"It went by so fast!" So many brides say this when asked to describe their engagement, wedding, or honeymoon. They become so overwhelmed by the details that all the wonderful moments before, during, and after the wedding become a blur. *Our Engagement Journal* is designed to help you to record all the events, thoughts, and feelings you experience from your very first date to your first wedding anniversary. It will encourage you to linger on moments you might have otherwise forgotten, lost sight of, or not known to expect.

Before you start writing, read through each section to get a feel for the entries. This will help you to stay tuned as you go through the phases of your wedding, so you can keep track of not only your emotions, but also details such as what you wore to the bridal shower, and what your honeymoon suite was like.

Approach the completion of sections collaboratively, as there are entries for the bride and groom to reflect on separately, and others that invite a joint response. You may find it helpful to reminisce with one another aloud before writing anything down.

Finally, try to fill in the journal as close to "real time" as possible, so that your responses are vivid and spontaneous.

When you're all done, you'll have a treasured keepsake to return to over the years. This special, romantic time in your life will be well documented, allowing your children and grandchildren to walk in your wedding-planning footsteps. Enjoy!

Beginnings

You'll never forget the moment when love came rushing in for the first time, or the magical day he asked, "Will you marry me?" and you realized that what all those stories had promised was true. Now is the time to record your memories of days you just didn't want to end—those early days when just thinking about each other would make your heart somersault, and even the cheesiest love songs seemed profound.

falling in love

HOW WE MET

_____

_____

_____

_____

_____

_____

_____

_____

_____

_____

_____

_____

WHERE AND WHEN

_____

_____

_____

_____

_____

_____

_____

_____

_____

_____

_____

_____

*"WE MET THROUGH A GROUP OF MUTUAL FRIENDS AT A
NIGHTCLUB. I THOUGHT HE WAS VERY CHARMING. WITHIN
FIFTEEN MINUTES, HE HAD ME SITTING ON HIS LAP!"*

—MARIA

HER FIRST IMPRESSIONS

_____
_____
_____
_____
_____
_____
_____
_____
_____
_____
_____
_____
_____
_____
_____
_____

HIS FIRST IMPRESSIONS

_____
_____
_____
_____
_____
_____
_____
_____
_____
_____
_____
_____
_____
_____
_____
_____
_____

our first date

WHEN
_____
_____
_____
_____
_____
_____
_____
_____
_____
_____

WHERE
_____
_____
_____
_____
_____
_____
_____
_____
_____
_____
_____
_____
_____
_____
_____
_____
_____
_____
_____

SHE WORE
_____
_____
_____
_____
_____
_____
_____
_____
_____
_____
_____
_____
_____
_____
_____
_____

HE WORE
_____
_____
_____
_____
_____
_____
_____
_____
_____
_____
_____
_____
_____
_____
_____

HOW IT WENT

OUR FIRST KISS

dating

RESTAURANTS

_____

_____

_____

_____

_____

_____

_____

MOVIES

_____

_____

_____

_____

_____

"OUR" SONGS

_____

_____

_____

_____

_____

_____

_____

PARTIES

_____
_____
_____
_____
_____
_____
_____
_____
_____

TRIPS

_____
_____
_____
_____
_____
_____
_____
_____
_____

MEETING THE FAMILY

_____
_____
_____
_____
_____
_____
_____
_____

favorite dates

SEXIEST DATE
_____
_____
_____
_____

FUNNIEST DATE
_____
_____
_____
_____

STRANGEST DATE
_____
_____
_____
_____

MOST FABULOUS DATE
_____
_____
_____
_____

MOST DISASTROUS DATE
_____
_____
_____
_____

MOST ROMANTIC DATE
_____
_____
_____
_____

the proposal

WHEN

_____

WHERE

_____

HOW

_____
_____
_____
_____

HE SAID

_____
_____
_____
_____

SHE SAID

_____
_____
_____
_____

THE RING

_____

_____

_____

_____

_____

_____

_____

_____

_____

SHARING THE NEWS

_____

_____

_____

_____

_____

_____

_____

REACTIONS

_____

_____

_____

_____

_____

_____

_____

_____

_____

All about us

Who are you? And now that you're engaged to be married, who will you become? As a couple, you've acquired a shared identity based on love, understanding, and common values, but now, as you forge a new life together as partners, remember that you are also individuals. Each of you has a personality, a family, your own goals, desires and beliefs. You have both been shaped by a host of unique stories and experiences.

all about her...

PARENTS

_____
_____
_____
_____
_____
_____
_____
_____
_____
_____
_____

THEIR WEDDING DAY

_____
_____
_____
_____
_____
_____
_____
_____
_____
_____
_____
_____

SIBLINGS
_____

_____

_____

_____

_____

_____

_____

FAVORITE CHILDHOOD MEMORY
_____

_____

_____

_____

_____

_____

_____

FIRST LOVE
_____

_____

_____

_____

_____

_____

_____

_____

FIRST DATE
_____

_____

_____

_____

_____

_____

_____

CLOSE FRIENDS

SPECIAL PEOPLE

FAVORITE...

COLOR

SMELL

FOOD

FLOWER

MOVIE

SONG

TV SHOW

BOOK

PLACE

GOALS

_____
_____
_____
_____
_____
_____
_____
_____
_____
_____
_____
_____
_____
_____
_____
_____
_____

DREAMS AND WISHES

_____
_____
_____
_____
_____
_____
_____
_____
_____
_____
_____
_____
_____
_____
_____
_____
_____

all about him...

PARENTS

_____

_____

_____

_____

_____

_____

_____

_____

_____

_____

_____

_____

_____

THEIR WEDDING DAY

_____

_____

_____

_____

_____

_____

_____

_____

_____

_____

_____

SIBLINGS

_____
_____
_____
_____
_____
_____
_____

FAVORITE CHILDHOOD MEMORY

_____
_____
_____
_____
_____
_____

FIRST LOVE

_____
_____
_____

FIRST DATE

_____
_____
_____
_____
_____
_____

*"MY PARENTS WERE ALWAYS KISSING.
SOME SATURDAY NIGHTS, I'D COME HOME
TO FIND THEM SWAYING TO THE ROLLING
STONES IN THE LIVING ROOM, PLATES OF
UNFINISHED CHINESE TAKE-OUT STILL
ON THE TABLE." —JESSE*

CLOSE FRIENDS
_____
_____
_____
_____
_____
_____
_____
_____
_____
_____
_____
_____
_____
_____
_____
_____
_____
_____
_____
_____
_____
_____
_____
_____
_____
_____
_____
_____
_____

SPECIAL PEOPLE
_____
_____
_____
_____
_____
_____
_____
_____
_____
_____
_____
_____
_____
_____
_____
_____
_____
_____
_____
_____
_____
_____
_____
_____
_____
_____
_____
_____

FAVORITE...

COLOR

SMELL

FOOD

SPORT

MOVIE

SONG

TV SHOW

BOOK

PLACE

"I KNEW SHE WAS THE ONE WHEN SHE AGREED TO PLAY GOLF WITH ME. IT WAS ONE OF OUR VERY FIRST DATES, AND SHE ALMOST BEAT ME... ALMOST!" —LEE

GOALS

_____
_____
_____
_____
_____
_____
_____
_____
_____
_____
_____
_____
_____
_____
_____
_____
_____

DREAMS AND WISHES

_____
_____
_____
_____
_____
_____

_____
_____
_____
_____
_____
_____
_____
_____
_____
_____

"I LOVE MY PARENTS' WEDDING PHOTOS. MOM LOOKS
SO YOUNG, LIKE A LITTLE GIRL IN HER NIGHTGOWN."
—DEBBIE

Celebrations

It's party time! In the run-up to your wedding, you've got a bridal shower to attend, the bachelor and bachelorette parties, and a rehearsal dinner (or welcome party) the night before the wedding. There's so much to look forward to—ribbon-wrapped gifts, fabulous food and cocktails, and, most importantly, an opportunity to bond with the people closest to you (or make insane amounts of mischief with them!). It's fun to relive these festive events, so be sure to document all the juicy details!

the bridal shower

WHEN
_____
_____
_____
_____
_____

WHERE
_____
_____

_____
_____
_____

HOSTED BY
_____
_____
_____
_____
_____
_____
_____
_____

THE INVITATIONS
_____
_____
_____
_____
_____
_____
_____
_____

THE GUESTS

FAVORITE GIFTS

REFRESHMENTS

FAVORS

FAVORITE MEMORIES OF THE BRIDAL SHOWER

the bachelorette party

WHEN

WHERE

THE GUESTS

THEY MADE ME WEAR...

THEY MADE ME DRINK...

JUST FOR FUN, WE...

_____

_____

_____

_____

_____

_____

_____

_____

_____

FUNNY MEMORIES

_____

_____

_____

_____

_____

_____

_____

_____

_____

FLIRTY MEMORIES

_____

_____

_____

_____

_____

_____

_____

_____

_____

_____

THE BEST PART...

_____

_____

_____

_____

_____

_____

_____

_____

THE WORST PART...

_____

_____

_____

_____

_____

_____

_____

_____

THE NEXT DAY I...

_____

_____

_____

_____

_____

_____

_____

_____

_____

the bachelor party

WHEN

WHERE

THE GUESTS

FIRST, WE MET AT…

_____

_____

_____

_____

_____

_____

_____

_____

_____

_____

THEY MADE ME WEAR…

_____

_____

_____

_____

_____

_____

_____

_____

THEY MADE ME DRINK…

_____

_____

_____

_____

_____

_____

_____

_____

_____

JUST FOR FUN, WE...

_____
_____
_____
_____
_____
_____
_____
_____
_____
_____
_____
_____
_____
_____
_____
_____

FUNNY MEMORIES

_____
_____
_____
_____
_____
_____
_____
_____
_____
_____
_____
_____
_____
_____
_____

FUNNY MEMORIES (CONTINUED)

_____
_____
_____
_____
_____
_____
_____
_____
_____
_____
_____
_____
_____
_____
_____
_____
_____
_____

FLIRTY MEMORIES

_____
_____
_____
_____
_____
_____
_____
_____
_____
_____
_____
_____
_____
_____
_____

THE BEST PART...

THE WORST PART...

THE NEXT DAY I...

the rehearsal dinner

WHEN

WHERE

THE GUESTS

"IT WAS AMAZING TO LOOK AROUND THE RESTAURANT AND SEE OUR ENTIRE LIVES IN ONE ROOM. EVERYONE WHO CAME EVENTUALLY FOUND THEMSELVES AT THE MICROPHONE MAKING A TOAST."
—ROBERT

THE MENU

_____

_____

_____

_____

_____

_____

_____

_____

_____

_____

_____

_____

_____

_____

_____

THE TOASTS

_____

_____

_____

_____

_____

_____

_____

_____

_____

_____

_____

_____

_____

_____

favorite memories

FUNNIEST MOMENT

_____

_____

_____

_____

_____

_____

MOST EMOTIONAL MOMENT

_____

_____

_____

_____

_____

MOST SURPRISING MOMENT

_____

_____

_____

_____

_____

MOST ROMANTIC MOMENT

_____

_____

_____

_____

_____

_____

"I REMEMBER HOW GREAT MY MOTHER
LOOKED AT THE REHEARSAL DINNER. SHE
WORE THIS YELLOW SILK SARI WITH THE RUBY
NECKLACE AND EARRINGS MY DAD HAD GIVEN
HER THE LAST TIME THEY WENT TO INDIA."
—RASHMI

Our wedding day

The big day is often a whirl of feelings, faces, and floral decorations, so it's important to tune into all the sounds, sights, and smells around you—the rustle of silk taffeta as you gather your skirts to walk into the ceremony, the sight of your grandparents jitterbugging on the dance floor, the warm, elegant smell of flickering candles. Soak it all in, be "in the moment," and have lots and lots of fun!

the morning of the wedding

THE WEATHER

_____

_____

_____

_____

_____

_____

_____

_____

THE BRIDE WAS THINKING...

_____

_____

_____

_____

_____

_____

_____

_____

_____

_____

THE GROOM WAS THINKING...

_____

_____

_____

_____

_____

_____

_____

_____

"I FOUND MY VEIL IN A LITTLE STORE THAT SPECIALIZED IN LACE CURTAINS AND VEILS IN BARCELONA. I FELL IN LOVE WITH THIS GORGEOUS MANTILLA, BUT IT WAS WHITE AND MY GOWN WAS IVORY. SO THEY DYED IT WITH TEA!"

—MELANIE

getting ready

THE DRESS

_____
_____
_____
_____
_____
_____
_____
_____
_____
_____
_____
_____
_____
_____

THE VEIL OR HEADPIECE

_____
_____
_____
_____
_____
_____
_____
_____
_____
_____
_____

SHOES

_____
_____
_____
_____
_____
_____
_____

JEWELRY

_____
_____
_____
_____
_____
_____

SOMETHING OLD, NEW, BORROWED, AND BLUE

_____
_____
_____
_____
_____
_____
_____
_____
_____
_____
_____
_____
_____
_____
_____

GETTING READY

MY BOUQUET

MOM'S REACTION

_____
_____
_____
_____
_____
_____
_____
_____
_____
_____
_____
_____
_____
_____
_____

DAD'S REACTION

_____
_____
_____
_____
_____
_____
_____
_____
_____
_____
_____
_____
_____
_____
_____
_____
_____

bridal party

THE BRIDE'S ATTENDANTS WERE

THE BRIDE'S ATTENDANTS WORE

_____
_____
_____
_____
_____
_____
_____
_____
_____
_____
_____
_____
_____
_____
_____

THEIR FLOWERS

_____
_____
_____
_____
_____
_____
_____
_____
_____
_____
_____
_____
_____

THE GROOM WORE
_____
_____
_____
_____
_____
_____
_____
_____
_____
_____
_____
_____
_____

THE GROOM'S ATTENDANTS WERE
_____
_____
_____
_____
_____
_____
_____
_____

THE GROOM'S ATTENDANTS WORE
_____
_____
_____
_____
_____
_____
_____

"WE PRACTICED OUR FIRST
DANCE ON THE MORNING OF
THE WEDDING. AFTER THAT,
I WENT SURFING."

—ANDREW

the ceremony

THE LOCATION

GETTING THERE

THE BRIDE'S ARRIVAL

BEFORE I WALKED DOWN THE AISLE I...

THE PROCESSIONAL

WHEN WE SAW EACH OTHER WE...

_____
_____
_____
_____
_____
_____
_____
_____
_____
_____
_____
_____
_____
_____

THE READINGS

_____
_____
_____
_____
_____
_____
_____
_____
_____
_____
_____
_____
_____

THE VOWS

THE KISS

THE RECESSIONAL

the reception

THE LOCATION

GETTING TO THE RECEPTION

GREETING OUR GUESTS

THINGS THEY SAID

the look

THE COLOR SCHEME

THE CENTERPIECES

THE TABLE LINENS

THE FAVORS
_____
_____
_____
_____
_____
_____
_____
_____

THE LIGHTING
_____
_____
_____
_____
_____
_____

THE WEDDING CAKE

THE TOASTS

THE MENU

_____
_____
_____
_____
_____
_____
_____
_____
_____
_____
_____
_____
_____
_____
_____
_____
_____
_____
_____
_____
_____

THE WINE

_____
_____
_____
_____
_____
_____
_____
_____
_____
_____
_____
_____

THE MUSIC

OUR FIRST DANCE

"I WAS FLOATING ALL NIGHT LONG, AS IF
I HAD ENDLESS ENERGY. THE NEXT DAY, MY
FACE HURT FROM SMILING SO MUCH!"
—VANESSA

favorite memories

FUNNIEST MOMENT
_____
_____
_____
_____
_____

MOST POIGNANT MOMENT
_____
_____
_____
_____
_____

MOST SURPRISING MOMENT
_____
_____
_____
_____
_____

MOST MAGICAL MOMENT
_____
_____
_____
_____
_____
_____
_____

the getaway

TOSSING THE BOUQUET

_____
_____
_____
_____
_____
_____
_____

LEAVING THE RECEPTION

_____
_____
_____
_____
_____
_____
_____

OUR WEDDING NIGHT

_____
_____
_____
_____
_____
_____
_____
_____
_____

The honeymoon

After the wedding, it's time to reconnect with each other in a place that's romantic, exciting, calming, intellectually stimulating...whatever you want or need it to be. Whether you embark on a nail-biting adventure in the wilderness, dance till dawn in a stylish city, or sun yourselves on a pink-sand beach, make time to luxuriate beneath the bed sheets, dozing in each other's arms. Enjoy every elegant, exhilarating, zany, sexy second of this incredible journey!

choosing the destination

OUR SHORTLIST OF POSSIBLE DESTINATIONS
_____

_____

_____

_____

_____

_____

_____

_____

OUR FINAL DECISION
_____

_____

_____

_____

_____

the journey

HOW WE GOT THERE

_____
_____
_____
_____
_____
_____
_____
_____
_____
_____
_____
_____
_____

ON THE JOURNEY WE...

_____
_____
_____
_____
_____
_____
_____
_____
_____
_____
_____
_____

"WE KNEW WE'D BE HUNGRY ON THE PLANE, SO WE PACKED UP HALF OF THE FIRST TIER OF OUR WEDDING CAKE AND ATE IT DURING THE FLIGHT."

—FELICIA

arriving

FIRST IMPRESSIONS

_____
_____
_____
_____
_____
_____
_____
_____
_____

OUR HOTEL

_____
_____
_____
_____
_____
_____
_____
_____
_____
_____

OUR ROOM
_____
_____
_____
_____
_____
_____
_____
_____
_____
_____
_____
_____
_____
_____
_____
_____
_____
_____
_____

THE VIEW
_____
_____
_____
_____
_____
_____
_____
_____
_____
_____
_____
_____

the first day

EXPLORING
_____
_____
_____
_____
_____
_____
_____

RELAXING
_____
_____
_____
_____
_____
_____

EATING
_____
_____
_____
_____
_____
_____
_____

*"A HURRICANE SET IN OUR
SECOND NIGHT AT THE RESORT,
SO WE DRANK BEER AND WATCHED
FROM OUR BALCONY. A WEIRD BUT
WONDERFUL ROMANTIC MOMENT."*
—KATIE

so much fun...

MOST DELICIOUS MEAL
_____
_____
_____

FAVORITE NIGHT OUT
_____
_____

SILLIEST ARGUMENT
_____
_____

FAVORITE ADVENTURE
_____
_____

SCARIEST MOMENT
_____
_____

MOST BEAUTIFUL SIGHT
_____
_____

LAZIEST DAY
_____
_____

FUNNIEST MEMORY
_____
_____

MOST PASSIONATE MOMENT
_____
_____
_____

SPECIAL PLACES

_____

_____

_____

_____

_____

_____

_____

_____

_____

_____

_____

_____

_____

_____

_____

_____

_____

PEOPLE WE MET

_____

_____

_____

_____

_____

_____

_____

_____

_____

_____

_____

_____

_____

_____

_____

_____

BOOKS WE READ

_____

_____

_____

_____

_____

_____

_____

_____

_____

_____

_____

_____

_____

_____

MUSIC WE LISTENED TO

_____

_____

_____

_____

_____

_____

_____

_____

_____

_____

_____

TOGETHER WE PLAN TO VISIT...

The first year

There's the first date, the first kiss, the first time someone says, "I love you." And now, the first year of marriage. Here, you'll highlight your favorite newlywed memories and milestones, such as your first anniversary, how you spend the holidays, and what your love nest looks like. Check in with yourself—and with each other—and use these last pages to lay out a plan for the future. Remember, the best is yet to come...

our first home

WHERE WE LIVE

_____
_____
_____
_____
_____
_____
_____
_____
_____
_____
_____
_____

WHAT OUR HOME LOOKS LIKE

_____
_____
_____
_____
_____
_____
_____
_____
_____
_____
_____
_____

entertaining

OUR FIRST DINNER PARTY

_____
_____
_____
_____
_____
_____
_____
_____

WE SERVED

_____
_____
_____
_____
_____
_____
_____
_____

WE INVITED

_____
_____
_____
_____
_____
_____
_____
_____
_____

HOW WE SPENT THE HOLIDAYS

OUR FIRST ANNIVERSARY

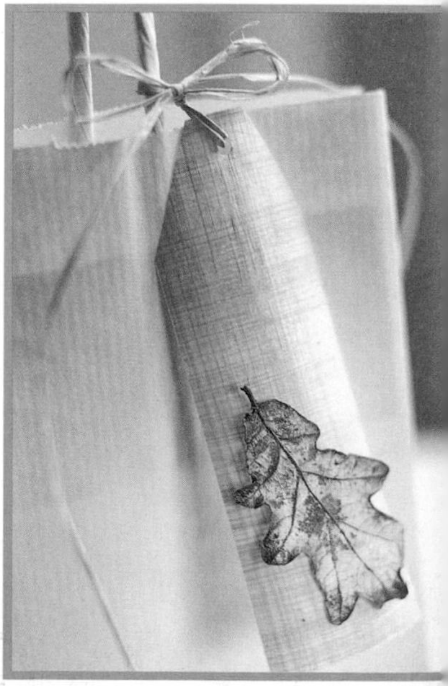

reflections

AFTER SIX MONTHS

_____

_____

_____

_____

_____

_____

_____

_____

_____

_____

_____

AFTER ONE YEAR

_____

_____

_____

_____

_____

_____

_____

_____

_____

_____

_____

_____

OUR HOPES AND DREAMS FOR OUR FUTURE TOGETHER

Photography credits
Key: a=above, b=below, r=right, l=left, c=center
Ali Allen front cover; Caroline Arber 45 inset; 58–61, 63; 88 inset; 92; 98; 144; Chris Everard 11;
Chris Tubbs 40 Phil Lapworth's treehouse near Bath; Christopher Drake 18–19; 26 Giorgio & Ilene
Silvagni's house in Provence; 116–117; Craig Fordham 6; 109–110; Dan Duchars 2; 25; 27–28; 31; 38;
46–47; 93; 95 inset; 106; 129; 132; 139; Daniel Farmer 1; 53; Debi Treloar 8; 32, 34–35; 50; 76; 131; 133;
135; Ian Wallace 14–15; Jan Baldwin 48–49; 111 & 136; Camp Kent designed by Alexandra
Champalimaud; 113–115; 118–121; 123-128; Peter Cassidy 20–21 background; 42–44; 45 background;
64–67; 107; Polly Wreford back cover; 3; 29; 4–5; 9; 16–17; 22; 24; 39; 51; 54–57; 70–73; 75; 77; 79;
81–87; 88–89 background; 89 inset; 90–91; 94–95 background; 96–97; 99–105; 108; 137; 140; Simon
Upton 122; Tom Leighton 36–37; William Lingwood 12; 20 inset; 21 inset; 68–69.

First published in 2006.
This edition published in 2016 by
Ryland Peters & Small
20–21 Jockey's Fields
London WC1R 4BW
and
Ryland Peters & Small, Inc.
341 E 116th Street
New York NY 10029
www.rylandpeters.com

Text by Amy Elliott
Text, design, and photographs copyright
© Ryland Peters & Small 2006, 2016

10 9 8 7 6 5 4 3 2 1

ISBN 978-1-84975-789-8

Printed in China

RYLAND PETERS & SMALL
LONDON • NEW YORK